*For Livinia*

# CONTENTS

**The numbers below correspond to poem number**

**See next page for CONTENTS (continued)**

# CONTENTS (continued)

**The numbers below correspond to poem number**

*Why* [1973]

Did you ever feel
That you were set upon the sea
Like a wave that would never come to shore?

Did you ever feel
That you would be alone
From now till evermore?

*Original Thought* [Jan 1985]

Today I forgot to read the newspaper
And began to sense
The rather surprising growth
Of original thought

*Unbelievable* [Jan 1985]

I can at times
So quickly flick
Or flip or fillip – if it could be called so
Or mathematically cusp
From being a christian
To being a practising atheist.
I know I've hurt you
My greatest friend of all.
It would be unfair
To use Peter as an excuse.

*Bubbles* [Jan 1985]

Let us explode
The bubble
Of class, mindset, unbelief, fixed knowledge
And 'reality'.
Let us allow
For some mystery
In this blessed life of ours.

Mind you,
We may discover another outer bubble.
But it will be fun bursting that one
And the many others that come our way,
If that is what bubbles do.

We may well choose the pin of laughter,
Or we may welcome, if need be,
The bitter sweet nail of suffering.

*Laughter* [Jan 1985]

Come to this well
And listen to some laughter,
Not a guffaw, or forced gladness,
Just simple joyous laughter
That sprinkles your heart
With hope.

Can you feel
That smile curving your mouth,
And the veil of slight sadness
Being lifted from your eyes,
And your mind beginning to sigh,
And your heart beginning to dance,
Not a wild jerky dance,
But a smooth flowing Staussian waltz?

Come to this well
And drink of some laughter,
But something may
Be asked of you,
Just a small something –
To begin with a smile.

*Heartbeat* [Jan 1985]

Let us allow beauty
To be brought forth in its own time.

Let us not tear
The heart of a tender spirit.
Let us not force words
That are not in season.
Let us not deny
The existence of pain and suffering,
More testing than awesome.
Let us not strain
The run of time.

Let us abide
With strength and gentleness
In the present.
Let us listen
With discerning eye
To the faint whisperings of wisdom.
Let us walk
In harmony with
The rhythmic heartbeat of life.

*Eastern Wind* [Jan 1985]

The eastern wind doth blow this way.
Hail, spray and snow doth play,
Whipping, stinging, needling my brow
Whilst the fire warms within.

*Water* [Feb 1985]

Water hardened
     Steely blue
Water softened
     Silvery grey

Water flowing
     Water sinking
In the sand of day

Water storming
     Water rising
Water frightening
     The air with spray

Water gushing
     Water rushing
Water cleansing

Water gurgling
     Water pure
Water quietened
     The wind at bay

Water nourishing
     Water soothing
Water smoothing
     The pain away

*Individuation* [Feb 1985]

Let us lift back the lid
And fly with strength
From normalcy, mediocrity
And despondency.
Let us not be afraid
Of striving to be our true selves.
And, if we wish to actualize,
To individuate,
Let us do it with gentleness
And with love of our neighbour,
And, though we take risks and face challenges,
Let us do so welcomingly and lovingly,
And, of course, with lots of courage.

*City Beach* [Mar 1985]

In the city
The rain powdered
Through wisps of smoke,
While, near the shore,
We drank in
The sound of the sea,
As gulls
Felt their flight wing
Curvingly, caressingly,
Beyond the sight
Of mindless eyes.

*Female Heart* [Mar 1985]

The female heart
Breathes in tears
Of listening
And breathes out
The breath
Of love.

*Leaving You* [Mar 1985]

The fire of my heart
Glows warmly.
I cannot force words
To shape a theme.
The glow may be
Like a sunset.

We are moving gently,
Calmly into night.
I wish you well
Allene.
I know it sounds final,
But we must cut
The cord,
And let the wind take us
Where it will,
Allene.
Farewell,
Good-bye.

*Fluffy Clouds* [Mar 1985]

Fluffy clouds attract,
But I'm afraid they bring sadness.
Let the sun shine on through,
The sky is bright and blue.

*Chemainus* [Apr 1985]

Broken chest,
Ripped,
Cracked through the bone,
See the heart.

Broken chest,
Ripped,
Cracked through the bone,
Feel the mind.

Broken chest,
Ripped,
Cracked through the bone,
Touch the tender soul.

*Taking Root* [Apr 1985]

Lift off,
Leave,
Fly away
Dream,
Choose the soil,
Grow.

Lift off,
Leave,
Fly away
Dream,
Prune the branch,
Flow.

Lift off,
Leave,
Fly away
Dream,
Rest the soul,
Know.

*The Nordic Why* [May 1985]

The Nordic why
Is losing its grip.
I am no longer chained
By a teeming mind.

*Synchronicity* [Jun 1985]

Sympathy, empathy,
Listening, sighing,
Aching, pulsing,
Breathing, needing,
Brother chair,
Sister table,
Brother tree,
Sister grass,
Brother fox,
Sister hare,
Brother man,
Sister woman,
Immanent force,
Emanating, drawing
Each to all,
All to each,
And each within.

*Language Class* [Jul 1985]

What,
    *I beg your pardon.*
Nice day,
    *Rather splendid morning.*
I belch after eating a lot,
    *I eructate.*
I make mistakes,
    *I err.*
That's wrong,
    *I believe that to be erroneous.*
I feel sad inside,
    *I feel a trifle downcast.*
I feel high,
    *I feel elated.*
That's bloody great!
    *Isn't that marvellous?*
I'm hungry,
    *I'm peckish.*
I get up in the morning,
    *I rise.*
I'm pretty smart.
    *I delight in my intellect.*
Hey!
    *I say!*
I'm proud of myself,
    *I have a healthy self-image.*
I sweat,
    *I perspire.*
I get angry sometimes,
    *Occasionally, I get irate.*
I make love,
    *I say! I make love too.*

*Flippancy* [Jul 1985]

Let go
Let go
Goodbye
Flip
Goodbye
Flippity flip

Take to the breeze
Now this way
Now that
Flow with the tide

Goodbye
Floppity flup

Your way
Mine
Hearts parting
Fingertips touching
Moving away

Now this way
Now that

I take off my hat
Won't turn back

Goodbye fluff
Goodbye fluppity flap
Flif flof
Goodippity flof
Flippity goodbye flof

*Sweet Abandonment* [Jul 1985]

Not so much consciousness,
Less thinking,
Sweet abandonment.

Less intellectualizing, rationalizing,
Sound of the psyche,
Sweet abandonment.

Letting energy flow,
Dissolving blockages with ease,
Sweet abandonment.

More who than what,
More being than effort,
Sweet abandonment.

More intuiting, sensing, feeling,
Allowing one's self to be loved,
Sweet abandonment.

Loving others,
Sweet abandonment.

Sweet, sweet,
Oh so sweet,
This taste
Of loving abandonment.

*A Butterfly Came Into My Room* [Aug 1985]

A butterfly came into my room
I was sitting on a chair

Thrice you came near me
And on the third time
Touched my ear

I held out my hand
But you would not land

I began talking to you
But you went your own way

I wanted you to feel my closeness
And come nearer

But mustard and black
Would not come back

My hand in the air
Waiting, waiting

But you would not land

At least you touched my ear
I do not know whether it was a whisper
Or an accidental flutter

A butterfly came into my room

*Brother Wolf* [Aug 1985]

I do not deny thee
Oh wolf within.
I hear the echo of your growl
In a far-off corner of my mind,
And in the bowels of my being.
The animal in me is still alive.
I will not be alarmed.

You may speak,
I will get to know thee and listen.

You may say what you will, brother wolf,
But, in the end, it is I
Who will decide what to do.

I do not deny thee
Oh brother wolf.

I do not deny thee at all.

*Mary Blue* [Aug 1985]

There is an icon of you,
Big eyes,
Small mouth,
Pondering things in your heart.
If I could but listen like thee.

There is a painting of you,
Flowing blue,
Pregnant,
Walking by the sea,
Full,
Human.
If I could but wait like thee.

*Yesterday Was A Dark Day* [Sept 1985]

Yesterday was a dark day
Though not stark black
The maudlin mood seamed
Through the mine of my soul

My heavy heart pounded
Sluggishly against my chest
My blood thickened
And flowed like oozing mud

My eyes, light-dimmed,
Fading to off,
Throbbed strainedly, smouldering
Half seeing, half blind

My mind became dull
And slowed to a crawl
Feeling, sensing pain
And little joy at all

Yesterday was a dark day
Though not stark black
I will walk on
And not turn back

*Gently The Heart Beats* [Sept 1985]

Gently the heart beats,
I hope you'll walk that way.
Silently the night keeps,
I see you dream again.

Dawn comes so soon,
And floats into noon.
If the eye be sound,
Well then, who knows.

Gently the heart beats,
To the time of day.
Gently the heart beats,
Hoping, come what may.

*Work* [Sept 1985]

*What do you do?*
    Well I breakfast.
*So, you are a breakfaster?*
    Well, I also breathe, walk
    Run, sweat, smile
    And get angry.
*But you look like a person with a practice.*
    Yes, that could be true,
    I practise living
    And am getting a little better at it now.

*But what do you do?*
*You must have a job!?*
    Are you asking me how much I earn?
*Now I don't believe I would do that.*
    Or are you asking me how I make my money?
*Yes, that would be closer.*
    Actually, I physicmentate.
*So, you are a physicmentator.*
    I also sit, stand, climb, sleep
    Scratch, listen, wonder, get sad and rejoice.
    Sometimes, I get really mad.

*Thank you for an interesting conversation*
*But there is one thing I'd like to ask you.*

*What exactly do you do?*

*Illusion* [Sept 1985]

I tried to grasp
A phantom of my mind,
And hold her tightly
Against my breast.

I saw her floating,
Rising slowly through the air,
Her body flowing curvingly,
Beckoning my heart from my breast.

My body sighed and pined,
Hungering for her aethereal love.
I blew a kiss into a vacuum,
And touched an empty core.

I walked towards her.
She did not wait for me.
Illusive, strange, compelling,
This haunting melody.

*Projectus* [Oct 1985]

Come home piercing arrows
Return to the bow
Of my heart and mind.

So oft'
From a seed sown
A flower grown
Too early plucked
Cut its scent
Thro' my friend's breast.

Come back oh you daggers
Re-enter the wound
From where you sprang
And though it may be painful
Let me willingly welcome
The children of this garden.

Come home you caging words
Uttered to cloak another
Yet truly mine
And for me alone.

The garden waits – trembling
Striving to be brave
Hoping to hear
An echo of some outer voice
And hearing instead
A rising cry
From the deepest roots of its soil.

*Water Stone* [Oct 1985]

At the centre of my being
There was a small powerful
Hardened stone, probably black,
Sapping my strength away.

It then came to me
That I would like a waterfall here.
But it must spring from the rock.

And so I gently dissolved,
For I like to be gentle,
The dull grey stone (if not black).
It disintegrated,
Powdering out of my mind's eye.

And in its place
A timid spring grew,
Until it gushed forth, with strength,
White foamy waters which refreshingly
Cleansed and smoothed the roughened,
Torn surface
Of my tender heart.

# The Expressive Mode

*Hermann Hesse* [Nov 1985]

O kindred soul
Who shows that sadness
Is merely the shadow of a cloud
I thank you.

O brother in heart
Who sees a young woman
As love's awakening
And not its end
I am glad for you.

O free man
Who allows
The coexistence of opposites within
I stand beside you.

O poet of the dawn
Who invites us
To be at home
In our own soul
I salute you.

*My Friend Time* [Nov 1985]

My friend time
Mends the wound
And restores to health again
In her gentle soothing way.

She applies the cream
Of days and weeks
To the bitterness
And sadness of the heart.

She clears the grime
That festers
In the distant parts of the soul.

My friend time
Plucks the arrowhead
From the centre of my breast
And gives my breath back to me.

She lifts the dark veil
That blinds me
From the love of others.

Loving time
Scatters and disintegrates
The dust of yesterday
From the far reaches of my mind.

O how I love you
My friend time.

*Liebesfrucht* [Nov 1985]

I am a spevum
Tender and alone
Being gently wafted
Through a channel unknown.

I emerge sensing
Into a larger space
Searching seeking
A loving resting place.

I am the fruit of love
Growing stronger
And more aware
With the passing of days.

I am helplessly fed
By a current of love
And a flow of blood
From without my warm membrane.

I am now ready
But yet hesitatingly emerge
Into a much larger space.

Yet again I yearningly
And achingly seek
A loving resting place.

*Love's Awakening* [Nov 1985]

Rusted nails
And dried blood
Swirl me
To the white fleece
In the blue of now

I become a white cloud
And feel the sun burn my heart
As I float unchained
On the winds of time

I am swept from the web of my past
Into the present
Plucking glass-fibre gossamers
From the moist morning grass
Of my soul

I begin to see my shadow
On the land of another
And shift
To let the sun trustingly through

I am a white cloud
And see my droplets
As tears of my mind
A heartfelt gnawing ache
Sad and joyful
Yearning to be loved
And to love
In the now of time

*Tread Lightly* [Dec 1985]

I would not cry it out aloud,
I might whisper it,
Inside to myself,
Perhaps.

I would not say it to others,
Unless carefully weighed,
Because I would be so afraid
Of being hurt (and I suppose of hurting).

Besides, I waver so often,
And am shy of language
About such things.

But I will say,
That, sometimes,
It appears crystal clear,
With an accompanying
Warm feeling inside:
And so,
Trembling, I gently whisper,
In spite of my many failings,
And, in my many loving tendencies,
That I long for and ache for
The mysterious Christ and
The God of Love.

*Poet* [Dec 1985]

I once more
Dip into the well,
And dare to say
I am a poet.

I hope
You like
To listen
To, at least,
Some of the music
Of my being.

And I hope
That I
Can listen
At least
As well as you.

*Early Morning* [Dec 1985]

Lady night lifts back her eyelids
Slowly dawns the day
Light spreads like a blanket
On a bed of shrouded clay

A whistling symphony of chirping friends
Breakfast first meal of the day
Fielded animals sleepily awake
Breathing spray
On the quivering green

Scented yellows, whites and blues
Sway in the morning breeze
A lone bee hums lowly
And on a flowering fuchsia feeds

Early morn waves her wand
Singing songs of colour to me
As Lady dawn slips forlorn
Kissing farewell to the whispering tree

*Long Before Dawn* [Jan 1986]

Long before dawn,
A man alone,
Soothes the pain
Of his heart,
And the suffering
Of his mind.

Cloaked and covered
In darkness,
On the brow of a hill,
Watching and waiting,
Restfully still,
He drinks
From a chalice of silence
Deep peace
Which fills
His lowly heart within.

Long before dawn,
He awakens the strength
To stand alone,
Building his mind, body, and spirit
To heal the sorrow,
And gladden the joy
Of another.

# The Expressive Mode

*Unwittingly Crushing / Hypersensitive* [Jan 1986]

Why do you tear me
To a future of yours
That is perhaps not mine?
Why do you force me
Into *your* projected
Pattern of development?

Could you try *not*
To squeeze me
Through the narrow strait
Of a previous
Experience of *yours*?

I know I am not whole,
Nor are you.
I know I am journeying,
As are you.

How is it,
You stir in me
The pain of being misunderstood?

You may some time
Hear me ask you,
Are you sure
You really listen?
Are you sure
You really feel for me
In the now of time?

*Priest* [Feb 1986]

How is it
A lamb is asked
To lead the sheep?
Why is it
The cry echoes
In my heart deep?

How strange
It must be
To leave all to gain all.
And what of
The wolf within the lamb
And the wolves among the sheep?

And what of
The need to lie
Beside a woman and hold her close?
And dare I
Answer the question,
What do I love most?

*Awakening* [July 1986]

A long time ago
A lone child
Fragile and frightened
Joined his hands
And bowed his head
As if to say a prayer.

O you out there love me
O you out there help me.

Then came a time
To learn to stand
A diamond cut thro' his breast
And a rod thro' his heart.

Rising still rising
Soiled clay
Crumbled and fell
Crumbled and fell
From his shoulders.

He stood firm and separate.

In this desert-land
He was aware of others
Standing at a distance

In an aloneness like his own.

# The Expressive Mode

*Waiting For An Australian Film To Come On TV* [Jul 1986]

Sometimes I pretend
To aspire towards humility,
But secretly, and indeed it may be no secret,
I wish to be famous.

I would like
A lot of people to admire me,
The archetypal hero,
And yet,
I claim to follow Christ.

Is it possible to have
A genuine desire
To be famous
For being humble!?

I, like my father,
Who died in June,
Would genuinely like to be
A saint.

I believe this to be
A fair enough aim.

My single goal is love
And love alone,
Thank you, Saint John.

Of course I falter,
But I'm great!
Cheers!

*What If!?* [Jul 1986]

What if
Each person is
More inclined to
Love than hate?

What if
Others ache
Knowingly and unknowingly,
To give and receive love,
As you do?

What if,
When you begin to give
You begin to receive?

What if
This love is real,
Eternal and
Here now?

Would all these things
Truly surprise you!?

*Get a Life* [Jan 1987]

Leave words.

Love.

Live.

Taste life.

*Get a Life* [Jan 1987]

*Our Time Of Need* [Nov 1989]

It is heartening to know of
A very poor person in a shanty area
Of Lima
Or living in a street
Near the 'house of the dying'
In Calcutta
Experiencing an inner urging
To come and be with the people
Of the Western World
In our time of need.

To accompany us
At this point in our history
To be with us
Without wishing to change us.

Who knows what will happen then!

*Light Blue* [July 1993]

I'm not racist
I like all colours
Not just black and white.

Look at me
Be attentive
Watch me
And listen.

Sit in your chair
And stare
Drink me in
While I
Mesmerize
Hypnotize.

Think what you like
To think you think.

You may speak
Your mind
Even if you have one
Of your own.

I can't hear you
I can't see you
And I'll let you be

I'm only your tv

*Growing Old* [Feb 1994]

How it came
I do not know
Came it did
I know for sure.

Befriend it?
Yes
For who can truly
Deny age?

Caught by surprise
A sidelong glance
Who owns this body
That has aged thus?

'Tis mine!, 'tis mine!

I turn
And face
The irrefutable
Unstoppable
Approach
Of dust.

*The Disappeared* [Oct 1994]

My voice
You can't hear
You can hear
An echo.

My face
You can't see
You can sense
An image.

My eyes
Life-twinkle
In your
Mind's eye.

My walk
I can't do
Without your
Memory.

Unbind
Keep me in mind
Releasing me
From nowhere.

*A What Without A Who* [Jan 1997]

Once upon human time
During a heated conversation
Among the word weary world weary
All of the words evaporated
And became a cloud of knowing
Which eventually rained liquid language
Into River Mellifluous

And my surprise
In the dumb deep silence
Was the great number of people
Who mistook the river
For the whole world

# The Expressive Mode

*a poem for Patrick Simms* [Nov 1997]

In meeting an other
Along with meeting the other
Perhaps we also meet
A lost part of our selves

And it is true, Patrick
That we will no longer meet you
On our walks through the hills

A rib-bone ache pains my heart
Telling me that in no longer meeting you
Along with no longer meeting that lost part of my self
It is *you* I will miss Patrick

*Regeneration* [2002]

Long lost
The feeling
As I write
Of deep things
Brought to light

A simple rhyme
That sounds fine
And is mine
Mine

Long lost
The route
To true
Light in my heart

Time again
To make
A start

Breathe in
Breathe out
Here it comes again
The word
And meaning
Of the word

What a delight
The light
To know
It's okay
To let
My feeling
Fleeting life
Expand

*Letter to The Irish Times* [2002]

I see that Fianna Fail*
And Winnie the Pooh
Have both recently celebrated
Their seventy-fifth anniversary.

Happy Birthday Winnie!

* The largest political party in Ireland in 2002

*Mountain* [2003]

What is it about a mountain
That draws us,
Like water,
From a well,
There,
On the edge
Of despair!?

What is it about the sameness of things,
As we grow older,
That blocks us, dulls us,
Breaks us,
Tempts us,
To give in,
To the lie,
That life's not worth living,
There,
On the edge ....

Yet not quite there,
Not quite there.

What is it about a mountain,
That gives us
Strength,
To look afresh,
At our lives,
Truly wondrous,
With newly opened eyes!?

What is it about a mountain!?

*Age and Grace* [2004]

Can a Club be iffy
About being fifty?
Not likely.
Perhaps needing
More craft on the crag,
But definitely not a drag.

Can we feel proud
In the shroud of a cloud
As we climb heaven-bound?
Maybe.

Can we talk the walk,
As we sometimes do,
Warm-glowing memory
Of boots in the sand,
Sky of ivory,
Rain- and sun-drenched land?
Perhaps we can.

More likely feeling nifty
About being fifty.
But can we climb?
Yes we can.

*Sweet Thursday* [Feb 2006]

Why is it of late
That Thursday
Has become
Sweet Thursday?

For nearly
Four weeks now;
Or has it been
Like this
For quite a while
And only now
I'm more awake?

Nearer to
The rest
From work
And other things

And sometimes
More electrifying
Than an over-waited-for
Friday evening

And were my life
But a week –
I am happily placed
On sound ground
Within sweet Thursday

For now

*Jack and Francis* [Nov 2006]

Charles Mitchell
Announced it on the news
In our two-storeyed house
Our white pebble-dashed
Blue-doored home
At the crossroads
In an eastern border-town

My mother came home
From Friday sodality
Saying everybody was crying
Especially the women
But definitely some men

The bare branches
Above the wall
Across the road
Blew this way and that
Scarecrowing the bleak November sky

Did he really have to die?

On another Friday evening
Six months later
At the same crossroads
With the branches
Furl-leafed and swaying
In a gentle May breeze
Francis rushed excitedly
Through Duffys' open gate
Into the way
Of an old Ford car
Leaving our family
Stunned and jarred

Mustard jumper
Light brown corduroy shorts
With slanted gold-zipped pocket
Long grey socks
Black Clarks' shoes
With design-indentations on the toes
Lovely blond hair and a big big head
Big enough to block Charles Mitchell
Reading the news about Jack Kennedy

*An Early December Walk* [Dec 2006]

Can anything good
Or anything at all
Come from
An early December walk
Walking past fields fenced
With haphazard wooden posts
Connected by
Smooth square-patterned wire
With a mesh sized
To frame a sheep's head
And on top
The prescribed single line of barbed wire

How much it has rained of late
Never seeming to stop
But it has stopped now

A gibbous moon lights up
Blackened hurrying clouds
Reminding me that the sun
Is there
Somewhere
Way way way
Back there

But there is an eerie feeling as I walk
As if I am being watched
By a hooded crow
Indifferent to my confident stride
And intake of breath

Isn't it a poor poor spirit
Who attempts to ingest
Some morsel of inspiration
From car lights
Reflecting off
The base of electricity wires
On a cold dark December evening
Such as this

*Primo Levi* [Jan 2007]

Still have I
The memory
Of stunned surprise
Thinking
How Primo Levi died

Did the curse
Of dark depression
Push him
Into a black hole
Where
He disappeared
By misadventure?

Or
Stating it bluntly
Did he kill himself
And that
An intended
Consequence
Of action?

How could
Such a tender writer
End his own life?

Was there
A deep deep
Guilt
In living
When
Others died
Primo Levi
Leaving Auschwitz
Laden with a
Vocation
To remind?

Did he slowly
Close his memory
Failing
To remind us
Of our forgetfulness
Then
Feeling the failing
Fell
Down down down
By metal-railed
Concrete steps
To the ground?

Is that how he died?

Or
Fairer still
A dizzy spell
With cruel farewell
Fell-swooped
Primo Levi
Five foot five
Thro'
A spiral stairwell

To a heartless end.

*Who More Can Tell* [Jul 2007]

Who more
Can tell
Where
One fell swoop
Of mortal pride
Will take us?

Unmasked,
I ask,
Is this life
All there is?

Whilst
Deep,
Deep down,
I hear
Another
Founding question
Sound –
Are we more
Than bones
In the ground?

*Somewhere In The Dark* [Jul 2007]

Somewhere,
In the dark,
In a secret cavern
Of my heart,
Am I mistaken,
To feel bidden
By a hidden
Heaven?

# The Expressive Mode

*The Expressive Mode / The Next Breath* [July 2007]

From Elliot Eisner
I have learned
The meaning of
The expressive
Mode of treatment of
A poetic form of representation

Deep structure
Moving beyond
The mimetic
The conventional
And beyond
Language itself

Does this
Make me
A better poet?

Hardly

Just as
I am
As alive as
My next intake of breath

I write well
Insofar as my next poem
Is well read

*Chinese Restaurant* [July 2007]

In Orchid Restaurant, Pembroke Road,
After some wine,
I asked my lovely Livinia
What stage her life was at:
A comma, a semicolon, a colon or a full stop?

She said
She felt her life
Had come to a full stop.

But it was really a semicolon:
Her life went on.

*Loss of Appeal* [Sept 2007]

Sickened by
The fascination
With celebrity,
And, in particular,
By the desolation –
*boredom, emptiness, sadness –*
Emanating from
The final year
Of a dying wasp's
Second term of office.

Media 'reality'
Where nobody
Becomes somebody
And, here, returns to
A lesser nobody
Than before.

Moses will rejoice!

At last,
The end
Of eight years
Where
Words from a Bush
Have had a clear and present
Loss of appeal.

# The Expressive Mode

*Herbert Park and Mother Nature* [Oct 2007]

Four young tufted ducks,

Sound-threaded to their mother,

Zigzag, swim and dive,

Beaded gold on sunlit fluff,

A pattern held fast when three.

*London is not England, Summer 1984* [Oct 2007]

I wanted to drive
Down thro' England
With purpose:
A friend, an English scholar, William,
Gave me his honeymoon route.

Cockermouth, a different William born,
Dove Cottage, that same William died;
Stood by Lake Windermere,
With paper and pen,
Not a word's worth.

Haworth, Brontes,
Looking thro' the window
Of the vicarage,
Feeling
Outside of things.

Stratford-On-Avon, another William again,
And, oh yes,
A visit to Chester and Chester zoo before that,
In a caravan on the front lawn
Of a B and B with lots of silverware,
Owned by Sarsfield,
And what's your first name?
That is my first name,
Sarsfield MacDonald,
His wife alive then.

A call to Oxford University
Along the way,
Peaceful, sunny,
Not overwhelmed,
And then on to London.

I ring my brother Bren
From a phone box.
Hello Brendan,
I'm in London.
Where are you?
I don't know.

I drive on,
Rolling down the left window
And then the right,
Three lanes of traffic,
Get directions.
Arrive.
Leave the Ford Capri
Outside my brother's house
For a week,
And back home
By the motorway.

*Four Months* [Nov 2007]

*July*

Early morning light
No children in the playground
Two squirrels at play

*August*

Friesian cow, swish swing
Of the tail, chews, moos, slow turns,
Brushes flies away

*September*

A tree in the lake
Full of cotton white egrets
Swirling mist rises

*October*

Star filled moonlit sky
Leaves rustle along the road
Hooded crows nearby

*Almost Free* [Nov 2007]

I am a gentle breeze,
Love laced with worry,
Feeling unworthy,
Yet loved immeasurably.

Will the time ever come
When I can truly say
No worry now?

I hear a tiger's fading heartbeat,
I see love torn and battered
Have its say.
I want to be in now here,
Loving, loved,
And breathe my way back
From nowhere.

I am a gentle breeze,
Love laced with worry.
Sometimes I feel oppressed,
But know a deep-felt strength.

I hold Elsie in my arms,
Hear her purr, and with her,
Feel happy, here now.

I worry too much at times
And cry when I am fatigued and stressed.

I am a gentle breeze,
Love laced with worry.
I understand some of the human mind, I think.
I say nonono to what's negative in papers and tv.

I try to live a life of love.
And keep on trying, even when I give up.

I am a gentle breeze,
Love laced with worry.

I am me,
Almost free.

*Snowshoeing* [Mar 2011]

Delighting in
The pleasure of climbing
In a sun-filled snowfall,
Fluffs of white floating
On a light breeze,
Wearing goggles for the first time,
I move with
Travellers through the snow:
Blue, red, mustard, pink,
Larch light and evergreen,
The rhythmic heartbeat of crunch crunch:
Lift the snowshoe, pause,
Engage, crunch,
Breathe, crunch,
Walk, crunch crunch:
Meeting a new found ground,
Impressing deep upon the mind,
The beyond-words of what I do,
Who I am,
And where we are,
Oft' forgotten, suppressed, submerged,
Oppressed,
But now stealing through the veil,
Into the crunch-crunch quiet,
Within a bowl of chamois-trailed snow,
Surrounded by Provençal Alpine peaks,
Never seen before,
Knocking at the mind's door,
Urging me to
Open my juniper-hidden heart,
And look out, route out,
A little and some more.

Made in the USA
Charleston, SC
14 October 2012